DINOSAUR

HUNT

DINOSAUR HUNT

TEXAS—115 MILLION YEARS AGO

KAREN CARR

A BYRON PREISS BOOK

HarperCollinsPublishers

ACKNOWLEDGMENTS

Many thanks and love to my husband and daughter, Ralph and Joanna Gauer, who always understand; to Gary Maxwell and Grammy, who make my work possible; and to my mom and dad, Bill and Linda Carr, for teaching me. Thank you to Deborah Diffily for her wonderful work and knowledge. Thank you to Howard Zimmerman, my partner in crime. And much appreciation and love to all the people in Texas who have shared their passion for dinosaurs with me.

Editor: Howard Zimmerman
Interior designer: Gilda Hannah
Display Typography: Stephanie Bart-Horvath
Jacket designer: Stephanie Bart-Horvath
Typeset in Badger
The art in this book was created using Corel Paint software.

A Byron Preiss Book

Library of Congress Cataloging-in-Publication Data
Carr, Karen.
Dinosaur hunt : Texas—115 million years ago / Karen Carr.
p.   cm.
Summary: Describes a prehistoric battle between two dinosaurs, based on fossil footprints found near the Paluxy River in Texas.
ISBN 0-06-029703-4 — ISBN 0-06-029704-2 (lib. bdg.)
1. Dinosaur tracks—Texas—Glen Rose Region—Juvenile literature.
2. Dinosaurs—Texas—Glen Rose Region—Juvenile literature.
[1. Dinosaur tracks.   2. Dinosaurs—Texas.]   I. Title.
QE861.6T72 C37   2002   2001039802
567.9'09764—dc21

Typography by Stephanie Bart-Horvath
1   2   3   4   5   6   7   8   9   10
❖
First Edition

To Louis Jacobs, who brought us together,

Dale Winkler, who gave us more on the Cretaceous than we could read,

and Jim Diffily, our dinosaur expert

INTRODUCTION

This book tells the story of a meeting between two dinosaurs. It is based on a series of footprints that were made 115 million years ago. Over time, the mud in which the prints were made turned to stone. Today, in Glen Rose, Texas, you can see the tracks made by the two dinosaurs. One was a *Pleurocoelus* (PLOOR-uh-SEEL-us), a large, four-legged plant-eating dinosaur. The other was an *Acrocanthosaurus* (ACK-roh-CAN-thuh-SAWR-us), a two-legged meat-eating dinosaur.

In 1938, a man named Roland T. Bird found large footprints on the bed of the Paluxy River, which is near Glen Rose. People who lived around there thought the tracks might have been from ancient birds, or maybe even bears. But Roland T. Bird recognized them as dinosaur tracks.

Mr. Bird followed one particular group of footprints and studied it for many days. He identified the tracks of an *Acrocanthosaurus* that run alongside twenty-five footprints of a *Pleurocoelus*. Then the footprints of both dinosaurs disappear under the bank of the Paluxy River. Mr. Bird found that both sets of tracks changed course at the same time. A missing left footprint of the *Acrocanthosaurus* might mean that the dinosaurs had collided with each other. Mr. Bird believed that the tracks tell a story. He thought they show signs of a dinosaur attack. Many scientists agree with him. They think this trackway is the sign of a meat-eating dinosaur attacking a plant eater, frozen in stone for all time: two dinosaurs in a battle for life and death.

That's what this book is about. The story of two dinosaurs that lived more than 115 million years ago, and what might have happened between them.

CAST OF CHARACTERS

Coloborynchus
kuhl-OB-uh-RINK-us

Pleurocoelus
PLOOR-uh-SEEL-us

Acrocanthosaurus
ACK-roh-CAN-thuh-SAWR-us

Baby
Acrocanthosaurus

Deinonychus
die-NON-ik-us

Tenontosaurus dossi
ten-ON-tuh-SAWR-us DOSE-eye

Hypsilophodon
hip-seh-LOFF-oh-don

It is 115 million years ago. This is the Age of Dinosaurs. It is a world totally different from ours. There are no human beings. The only mammals are tiny, mouselike creatures. Dinosaurs dominate the earth.

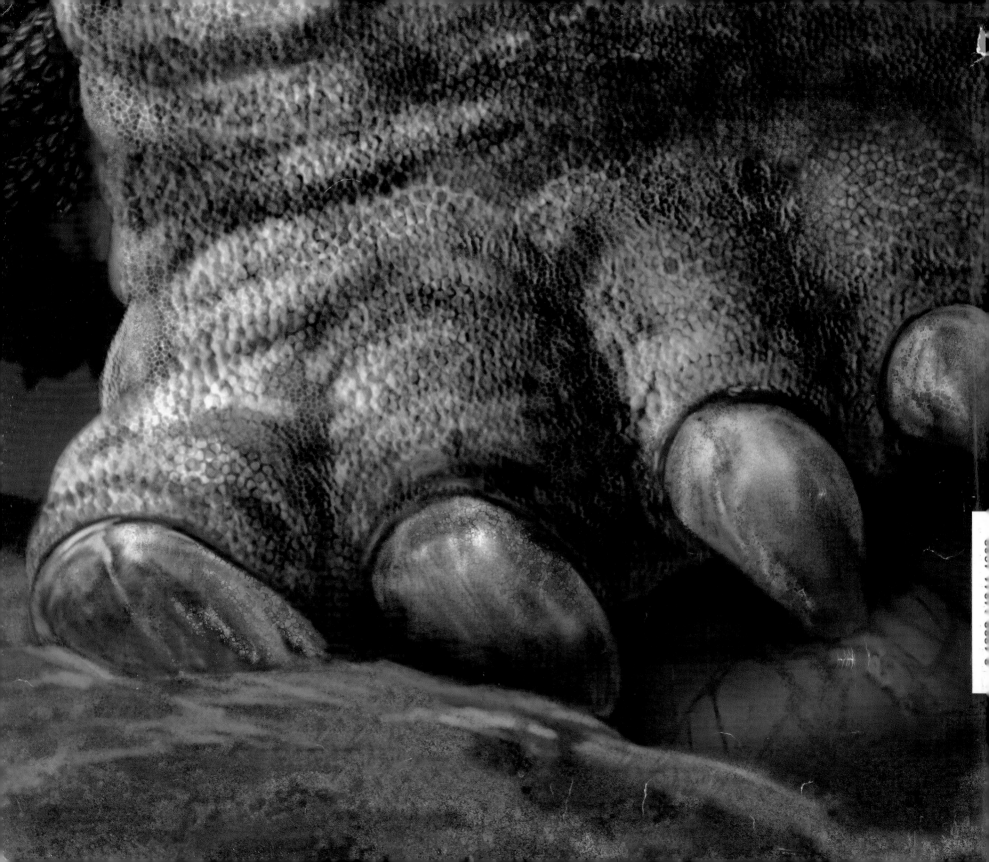

Some of the dinosaurs are huge. Some are small. But no matter what their size when fully grown, all dinosaurs begin life as babies. This one is just hatching.

It is a baby *Acrocanthosaurus.* Her mother is not there to help, and she is all on her own. When she grows up, she will be feared by many other animals. She will hunt and eat small dinosaurs, reptiles, and mammals. But now she must figure out how to find food without being eaten herself.

Alone in the forest, the baby dinosaur looks around her world. She sees green plants—ferns and cycads—and tall trees that have sharp leaves. Beyond the forest, the *Acrocanthosaurus* glimpses a shallow sea. When the tide is low, mud flats stretch between the water and the forest.

The baby dinosaur is hungry, but she cannot eat the plants she sees. *Acrocanthosaurus* is a meat eater. At first, she catches insects that buzz by her head.

Still hungry, she searches for snakes and small lizards and mammals that she can kill easily. The more she eats, the stronger she grows. But as she gets larger, she will need more and more food.

The young dinosaur watches fully grown acrocanthosaurs hunt for food. She sees them use their sharp teeth and pointed claws to kill big animals, like other dinosaurs. The young one tries to do this, too.

She spies a dinosaur just a bit larger than herself. It is a *Deinonychus*. She begins to chase it. But this dinosaur is a meat eater, too.

The *Deinonychus* fights back. His sharp claws dig painful scratches along the *Acrocanthosaurus*'s neck. Bleeding and in pain, she gives up the chase. She is still hungry, but she has learned a valuable lesson. She will now look for smaller dinosaurs to eat. Every time she hunts, she learns something new.

In a few years, the young *Acrocanthosaurus* has become a successful and deadly hunter. She has learned that she can attack big dinosaurs if they are old or sick.

She has learned to approach from behind and attack her prey using teeth and claws. And she has learned where to bite an animal to bring it down quickly.

Now fully grown, the *Acrocanthosaurus* knows she must be a careful hunter. She is 12 feet high, 30 feet long, and weighs 6,000 pounds. But one kick from a larger dinosaur could still break her bones. And if she is wounded, she may not be able to hunt. Not hunting means not eating.

The *Acrocanthosaurus* is hungry once again, and her stomach growls. She spies a young *Pleurocoelus* walking along a muddy stretch of land between the forest and the sea. The *Acrocanthosaurus* stays in the forest, hidden by the trees. She follows the young plant eater as quietly as she can.

She watches the *Pleurocoelus* closely. He is alone. She thinks he may be lost. Usually, he would be with other dinosaurs of his kind. He is walking slowly and he may be sick. Still, the *Acrocanthosaurus* will need to use everything she has learned about hunting when she attacks this large dinosaur.

Still hidden by the forest, the *Acrocanthosaurus* shortens the distance between herself and the plant eater. When she is close enough, she darts out of the trees and onto the mud flats. She races after the large dinosaur and lunges at him. Using her razor-sharp teeth, she bites into the skin near his front leg. She sinks her teeth in deeply, and holds on.

In pain, the *Pleurocoelus* shifts his heavy body. His attacker is lifted off the earth. The *Acrocanthosaurus* releases her bite and falls to the ground. The *Pleurocoelus* kicks at her but misses. He tries to run away, but she chases him. She is faster, and he is wounded. She attacks again.

This time, the *Acrocanthosaurus* uses her front claws and all of her 60 sharp teeth to attack her prey. Carefully staying away from his whipping tail and kicking feet, she continues to claw and bite. Soon, the *Pleurocoelus* is bleeding from many wounds.

The *Acrocanthosaurus* moves back, away from the kicking legs, and watches her victim. The *Pleurocoelus* is too weak to run anymore. He tries to walk, but cannot. Severely wounded, he slowly dies. The *Acrocanthosaurus* moves closer and begins to feed on the dead dinosaur. She can have a big meal now, but there is still danger.

The *Acrocanthosaurus* has to protect her
food from other meat-eating dinosaurs.

While she is eating, another adult *Acrocanthosaurus* and a *Deinonychus* try to bully her away from her kill. They want to eat, too. And sometimes stealing a meal is easier than

The *Acrocanthosaurus* rushes the other meat eaters. Each time she charges at them, they move away. When they are at a safe distance, she can eat again. She must defend her food, or it will be stolen away.

It is now six hours after the *Acrocanthosaurus* first
saw the *Pleurocoelus* moving slowly along the mud
flats. She walks back into the forest to sleep. She
does not have to hunt for a few days now. Her
stomach is full, and she can rest.

But soon, she will be hungry again. She will have to hunt for more food and that means hunting another dinosaur. If she is successful, she will live long enough to mate and lay her own eggs. Some of her children will perish, but some will survive. And the cycle of dinosaur life will continue.

Two dinosaurs left their footprints in the mud 115 million years ago. The tracks of the *Acrocanthosaurus* and the *Pleurocoelus* are still there today for all to see. After all this time, we can look at the trackway, now turned to stone, and imagine how one dinosaur must have lived, and how another may have died.

A NOTE FROM THE ARTIST

While my subject matter for *Dinosaur Hunt* was ancient life, the technology I used to create the illustrations in the book is pretty up-to-date: I paint on a very large graphic workstation, using a paintbrush-like stylus to draw and paint the images. All of the images you see in the book were painted in traditional oil paint and watercolor styles, using Corel Painter 6, a software package that beautifully mimics the canvases and media painters use. While I really enjoy traditional oil painting, "digital" painting gives me the same freedom to layer and play with color—without having to wait for it to dry! You can find a lot more about how I make pictures using "electronic paint," and you can send me comments or questions, at my web site: www.karencarr.com.

Photo by Carolyn Brown

Artist Karen Carr's mural of an *Acrocanthosaurus* attacking a *Pleurocoelus*. It is on display at the Fort Worth Museum of Science and History. It is ten feet long and seven feet high. Karen based it on the fossilized trackway the dinosaurs left in the mud flats of Texas. That's Karen herself, peeking in at the right.